# math for couples

## ESSENTIAL POETS SERIES 242

**Canada Council
for the Arts**   **Conseil des Arts
du Canada**

**ONTARIO ARTS COUNCIL
CONSEIL DES ARTS DE L'ONTARIO**

an Ontario government agency
un organisme du gouvernement de l'Ontario

Canadä

Guernica Editions Inc. acknowledges the support of the Canada Council
for the Arts and the Ontario Arts Council. The Ontario Arts Council
is an agency of the Government of Ontario.

We acknowledge the financial support of the Government of Canada.
*Nous reconnaissons l'appui financier du gouvernement du Canada.*

# math for couples

ADELE GRAF

**GUERNICA
EDITIONS**
TORONTO • BUFFALO • LANCASTER (U.K.)
2017

Michael Mirolla, editor
David Moratto, cover design, interior design
Guernica Editions Inc.
1569 Heritage Way, Oakville, (ON), Canada L6M 2Z7
2250 Military Road, Tonawanda, N.Y. 14150-6000 U.S.A.
www.guernicaeditions.com

Distributors:
University of Toronto Press Distribution,
5201 Dufferin Street, Toronto (ON), Canada M3H 5T8
Gazelle Book Services, White Cross Mills, High Town, Lancaster LA1 4XS U.K.

First edition.
Printed in Canada.

Legal Deposit—First Quarter
Library of Congress Catalog Card Number: 2016959323
Library and Archives Canada Cataloguing in Publication

Graf, Adele, 1944-, author
math for couples / Adele Graf.

(Essential poets ; 242)
Poems.
ISBN 978-1-77183-195-6 (paperback)

I. Title.  II. Series: Essential poets ; 242

PS8563.R3148M38 2017      C811'.6      C2016-907229-0

*for my family
and for Ed*

# coordinates

a graph
A. Graf
Ma Graf
*ma griffe*
myself
auto-Graf
autograph
Adele Graf
a *belle* Graf
a bell graph
Adeley with graffiti on her belly

    *—Adele Graf, 2017*

# Contents

## I. Sorehenna: *as her, none*

## II. outside quotidian time

## III. half moons

## IV. Moorside Blend

**Sorehenna:** *as her, none*

# on seeing Picasso's
# "Woman in a Hat with Flowers"

when I was one week old, Picasso painted my life—
its untainted canvas white
to heighten my colours as they emerged

his cubist perspective recast
my young self after my father's death
and my mother's collapse to mourning

he striped my dress with white and gold
but raised its pointed neckline high
to constrict my throat and mute my voice

he detached my right arm from my shoulder
since he knew that loss would unhinge
and strand me from support

I'd seethe long before love softened me
so my black hair defines red triangles—
fierce pigment for my mother's grief

he moved my white mouth to my cheek
when he saw my face skewed in stress
with no parents to shield me

then he named his work for my milliner
grandmother, whose warmth healed me
as if she'd sewn his flowers on my hat's mid-brim

her joy and his painting outlast fleshed hands—
she joins her contemporary Picasso
to shape my glad red hat

# Swee-Touch-Nee

I share a cup of tea with my grandmother
who's been dead for forty years —
she rises as I split the wrap
on my Swee-Touch-Nee tea,
its flat orange box, mustard trim
like the gilt and crimson
tin treasure chest
her tea came in then —
"The Aristocrat of Teas"

a child, I sat at her kitchen table —
enamel white metal, white wooden chairs,
drank milky tea from squat glass cups,
dunked sugar cubes —
now it's I who fill the cup she lifts
unsteadily, stir it sweet and white

I share a last meal with my grandmother
often, on any occasion —
I gently slide her scalloped
ecru plates from my shelves,
remember to serve vegetarian food
on these, her *milchig* dairy plates,
set out homemade soup in her last
two unmatched ecru bowls,
prepare a batch of *blintzes* to show
I still use her serving platter

we eat side by side
in my brick-walled nook,
here at my kitchen table
where I offer her the soft chair

# Sorehenna: *as her, none*

childhood flies home in dreams
to my grandmother's cramped fragrant rooms
on sounds of synagogal melody

*ne'er a nosh*
    her meals brimmed with cool
pink summer borscht, chopped liver
toasted mounds, oblong braided bread
served in sun, her head held high

*sane her, no?*
    warming to grandchildren who
nimbly skipped from Yiddish tradition
she stuffed nuts and pears in Christmas
stockings hung on protruded knobs
of her broad split-level stove

*an' her nose*
    prominent but eclipsed
by smiles, smelled blended scents in rooms
behind her store (paste wax–antimacassars–
humid sills) that my nostrils still retrieve
from burnished wood when nights are warm

*near shone*
    her face, as now when breezes
of remembrance flutter over her, ensconced
in flowered sunshine of some imagined later
home as full and pleasing as her own

*hens are on!*
 Sundays her closed store —
sole space wide enough to welcome all —
transformed once guests who'd helped
to spread her narrow table circled round
for slow-roasted chicken dinners, children's
gifts stitched from velvet ends

*earn she? no!*
 as she waited for clients
in her passé milliner's shop —
pink footstool near her window display
where her foot on the stool
then knee in the window brought hats within reach —
this footstool, later muted beige
now eases my aged feet

*ha, sneer on!* or *ah, no sneer!*
 too late to tell her, I can soar
to where she hovers near my skin —
from her auburn hand-held mirror
my own old woman's face stares at me
but after years of hugs and pangs
Sorehenna's joy runs through my veins

# Greek island legacy

each spring my grandmother returns to me
reborn as the season wakes — I find her
where wildflowers bloom, even on the high path
atop the bastioned walls of Rhodes, amidst

airy Queen Anne's Lace, swaying on slim stems
bunches of perky vermilion poppies
daisies, fields of them, their yellow
spilling onto petalled whites

once these flowers took her back to childhood
meadows, now they remind me of
my sun-filled youth with her —
she enfolded me as these walls enfold this town

till one night she faded
at her season's end, then bequeathed
her presence in this wild array
whose blossoms welcome her again

today she stays near me, sunlight
in her eyes, as Queen Anne's Lace holds light
within its wide white cluster —
her smile, like polished poppies

gladdens this path worn smooth —
even now, our fingers touch
as she helps me braid a daisy chain
for my own granddaughter's hair

# tonic

*for my grandmother*

sea air you breathe bathes your spirits
so once back home, you can harbour
worries that wash up with each new year's tides

bright pink sea roses start you singing
smooth surf soothes your year-round rush
from meals to your store, where sales trickle in

salt water binds last year's wounds, restores
your strength to call on sick Mrs. Arnowitz, aged
Florence Belsky, then to bake a *challah* for lame Mr. Weiss

alone, in your faded Latvian apron
you insist that your week of tangy air
keeps you on the visitor side of the sick room door

# harmonious arc

my concert companion Frank
always arrives in the hush
before the downbeat falls
and music begins

he needs no seat, happy to hover
overhead, lulled as we share
the sound's perennial splendour
through raised hairs on my skin

he grasps even more nuanced
pitch and phrases, now that his ear
bones and cavity have lost
their muffle of former flesh

violinist Frank silently explains old
techniques that burnish the tone
then I wordlessly brief him on
this century's performance style

he describes Mischa Elman's playing
to me; I tell him of Gil Shaham — but mostly
we form a harmonious arc from the stage
through his air to my seat

once my grandfather Frank's small
immigrant body stood each day
in his corner store, his large ears
straining toward melody

his mind rode horseback through
Latvian pines, his fingers recalled
violin tunes as he awaited
his annual treat —

early 1900s, nickel carfare, standing room
high in Carnegie Hall to hear Mischa Elman
whose feats he later recounted
for his clustered family

now this man I never met, barely know about
soars to see his love of music still alive
in me, while I, who can attend
fine concerts on a whim

listen as Frank, skimming his dead century
tags along, in case one day
he plucks his own ethereal strings
or bows me his own song

# On Bergenline Avenue

*in West New York, New Jersey*

Brakes still sigh at 54<sup>th</sup> Street:
my feet touch Bergenline.
The bus took side streets from fifty
years ago, dense houses then
tarred in shingles now vinyl-sealed.

Rispoli's rusted sign swings
above the vacant bakery.
I tell the young realtor
I can taste their plum tarts.
He says *a long time ago.* I flinch

from flapped squawks
in the poultry market where
kosher chickens ran headless.
A new owner stands in the same
feathered stench.
*Been here long*? I ask.
He shakes his head.
*No entiendo.*

At 5405, the man at Mina's
Dollar Store chats in scant
English. Yes, his building was once
a Cuban cigar store. Before that?
Has he heard of my grandmother's
hat shop, there for forty years?

Up two stairs behind her store,
the three rooms we lived in
gutted into Mina's.
A cardboard sign warns
*WATCH YOUR STEP*
here where the floor still slopes up.
The man shrugs, wraps
the memento pen I buy,
his palm outstretched for 99¢.

Windows darken
on my bus ride home.
Through the drape between
Grandmother's rooms and store,
her lamp glows. I watch her climb
two stairs and sit on the pink plaid couch.
In her lap, a grosgrain hatband.
She embroiders my name.

# welcome

one nickel
in her milliner's till
nothing saved behind

near noon
when a friend stops by
of course
Gram offers lunch

she crosses to the grocer
& buys sardines
for their meal

cost of the can: 5¢

# empty green storage box

1.
slanted like old German script
Grandmother's handwriting
on the white label framed in gilt

tongue clucks as she searched
for glasses to perch on her nose
but her arm aware

of where the green box she wanted
sat among rows of boxes
four across and five high

thin iron handle dangling
from the frame, her middle fingers
lifting it level to pull the box out

the handle's release
onto solid cardboard
its click like a door knocker


2.
spools of silk and velvet ribbon
piles of taupe and dark veils
starched roses, curled feathers, satin bows

velour hat brims she'd learned to shape
as Herr Behrmann's apprentice
when she had to leave school

elastics to secure straw hats
like those she'd sold for Aunt Fayga
in 1902 at the Tukums fair

whiff of mildew inside this box
otherwise unblemished
by a hat-maker's scissors and thread


3.
ornate frame for its label punched
through cardboard, back flanges
splayed under white cloth tape

paper veneer glued firm, front corners
frayed, colour faded except where
covered by the label and lid

the set of rectangular boxes
good value in 1925 for a widow
outfitting her own milliner's shop

whose last box even now might yield
the pearl-tipped hatpin
my fingers seem to stroke

# Grandmother's mountain meadow

was it like this for you, Grandmother?
your meadow's breezy stillness curved to distant pines
its grassy quilt sewn with bright dots and patches —
low purple lupins, yellow buttercups
wide white thimbleberries
and high above the rest, singly or in throngs
golden daisies, whose petals circle crimson mounds
dainty low-lying bluebells
splashy pink wild roses that hold the buzz of bees

if this was your girlhood field
what boundless calm you breathed
your outspread hours
far-flung spaces
infinite in your eyes

I sit among these flowers
near a brown park sign planted here
to help me understand this vista —
its *drumlinized hills, ridge-like kames*
*glacial moraine* and *evolving fescue* —
though geologic terms intrude
on my inward view of simpler times
festooned with floral colour that swirls back to you
as I scan the sign for lore you might have known

I'm just a tourist
learning that the flowers and grass
feed elk, deer and mountain sheep
in this landscape that revives
your hushed childhood home

# lexicon of travelling light

**backpack:** pared to 1960s student trek essentials, including Sartre's books (even this cool Existentialist wouldn't declare these *de trop*)

**corsage:** boosted my breezy takeoff to a farewell gala, as my grandmother pinned her gift on my *de rigeur* plain shirt

**finery:** negated my "hip" unstudied outfit, when my proud Gram lingered nearby in her milliner's hat with clasped purse

**homemade cookies:** handed by Gram as last-minute baggage (couldn't she see that my young ideas had no room for her old-world ways?)

**modernism:** jettisoned the corsage on board, then devoured the cookies to lighten my load (Sartre himself would have salivated at their creamy centres)

**nostalgia:** now kindles twenty-first century warmth for my Gram, who baked those cookies and bought that corsage with quarters and dimes

**philosophical shift:** regresses from Sartre to Plato, whose "universal forms" of long-wilted corsages (beyond specific carnations or orchids) and "ideal" once-creamy cookies (beyond butter or cream-cheese filling) lead me to realize my grandmother embodied the supreme "form of the good"

**regret:** compounds annually for the squandered soft spot my grandmother offered

**savvy:** kneels no more to now-passé Jean-Paul, nor to today's icons

**suitcases:** accumulate for years, as I stuff them with what I'd once deliberately discarded

# elasticity

*for my daughters*

heart-strings and blood
formed the cord
that nourished you
links our innards
through the years
stretches from telephone
pole to pole
curls close to your mouth
as you absorb maternal lore
plumps to dough I roll as we chat
thins to noodles for your soup
flows on in the cord
you now share with your own

# splashy jazz

dinner done, long day's summer heat still a hum
our toes inhale the dusk, drag it deep inside our legbones
plunged in a plastic pool, dousing our torsos with showers

in upper register, our xylophone piece unfolds —
my small granddaughter's legs cavort in rhythm we imitate
(*staccato* splash interspersed with prolonged *legato*)

my older granddaughter's legs kick in, mallets
that hammer and caress the liquid instrument
with syncopated sway that we (the back-up band) repeat

lower pitched, my daughter's legs begin their riff—
a fanfare beat replete with measured spray
and finale the younger set extends in *ritardando*

till my matriarchal legs leap to join these offspring
of shinbones and thighbones, our long thin legs
keeping cool time in lanky harmony

# anatomy ↔ genealogy

*for Kaia*

**her genesis**
my two-year-old descendant
two generations down
draws two faint meandering circles —
first: small radius, placed below
second: larger rim, set above
yet the first supports the second
where their lines converge —
then two more circles:
small circumferences, equidistant
high inside the second sphere

**her hypothesis**
first circle: belly button

**my analysis**
primordial navel
coiled cord that ties us
to our forebears
leads us to our heirs
from me to her
from her to those who propagate
her wisdom

**her hypothesis**
second circle: head

**my analysis**
derivative head
offshoot of the generating navel
spacious skull packed with
curling pathways that
connect generations
from history to discovery

**her hypothesis**
last two circles: eyes

**my analysis**
subsidiary eyes
transmitters of our sights to
neurons nestled in
our heads, whose
visual memories
enrich each new view

**my synthesis**
superfluous appendages
neck   arms   legs
just to drift about
hair   eyebrows   lips   cheeks
just to decorate —
the navel carries us
backward and forward
to round out our family line
the head sees with understanding

# Aristotle's friend

*for Anna*

*once upon a time*, the girl
begins, brown eyes bright
*there was a rabbit named Rabbit*

*& Rabbit ate a carrot*
*& then she hopped & hopped*
*then she went home &*
*her mama·opened the door —*
*the end*

the girl knows the essentials
of the genre — beginnings
middles, ends — from all
the varied stories she's heard
in her two years of life

already, she's best of friends
with Aristotle, born
two thousand years ago
& a thousand times her age

# A toddler learns language

*for Ben*

Look at this park bench
with a woman and child
like you two who ate Triscuits
and pears. Your toddler points
to the picture in his second
bedtime book and says
*That's you and me.*
Fingers linked, you ran
to the sandbox, called each other
*Button* and *Bagel*, filled his pail
at the fountain again.
You sang "Baby's Boat,"
plopping cheese cubes
onto his tongue. Now he's chosen
blue pyjamas, you've tickled
his skin where the diaper slid.
Remember when he hid near
the green chair and you
crouched behind the hall door?
His lips and tongue form
the words, around index and
middle fingers in his mouth,
his eyes bright as a miner's
who emerges from bedrock with gold.

# granddaughter, age 3

*for Kaia*

cabbage rolls hurt her brain, she says
science behind it like this —
bubbling burps form in her belly
rise through her body
rest in her brain

each cabbage roll she eats
strengthens & speeds
these burps to her brain cells
lengthens their cerebral life
pain negating her palate's pleasure

but where else could they go?
we query, when cabbage rolls
you feast on
equal your body weight

# signature

*for Anna*

Mr. Floop still feeds his lunch to parkland pets
(breadcrumbs to birds, peanuts to squirrels, sausage to dogs)
then eats the bread, nuts and wurst a kindly matron shares —
the llama goes on searching for her mama
quizzes animals she meets to learn her ancestry

these books now hold their stories within —
quietly stacked since you've gone, your high spirits
renaming yourself *Willowfrost*, me *Turteler* —
your whirlwind spent as you left my house
to sleep your way home ... still on my shelf
one smiling dinosaur sticker
with glittered green scales, red tongue
and your gift of your first signature

turquoise marker bobbed as your hand worked
to master it at my kitchen table, dark eyelashes
down, turquoise ink on your lower lip —
mile-high letters you wrote from right to left
spell your palindrome name, *Anna*

outside quotidian time

# lightly up and over

dormant kernels clatter down the steel bin
jostle headlong, rush to mingle
tremble when warmth they've never known
flows from below

then each releases its aroma

their shared scent
stirs the corn to yearn
for bliss its hardness
has barred it from so far

*pop* — one bursts into white bloom

others sense softness in their skin
nestle in the throng of open corn
that levitates, touched by
such close contact

now their inner grain takes shape

but from below *pops* accelerate
new kernels surge on air
nudge the high corn through the chute
over the edge, into cold bowls

a brief flowering dashed with salt

# From my warm oiled water
# to her wall-frame photo

I'm reclining full-length in my clawfoot bathtub
when my young self and I lock eyes. Flat behind glass,

she soaks in the short clawfoot tub at her student house.
Her hair, darker than mine, piled above the water.

Her smooth hand, with a wedding band, presses
her novel's page. She faces the lens as if I might speak.

I abstain. Veins in my slackened flesh still merge
with hers, so I'll wager she wants her book,

not my answers to questions she doesn't have —
whether her new husband strays, if Fellini

becomes passé, which nation feels like home,
how often she sees sons who have grown.

Inside our silence, my own thoughts converse.
They answer the question I didn't know I had.

Despite my skin's sag, what she's got that I crave
is only her bounty of countless days.

My time pinches as I glimpse its cramped end.
Her outspread time pulses as she dallies.

# October 5, 1957

What changed the world last night?
Mr. Briggs asked our Grade 8 class.
Russia and *Sputnik I*.

I was like Laika the dog
when she spun in *Sputnik II*
outside her simple world.

Mr. Briggs explained our country's
excitement, our fear of a new era.
He talked of expanded frontiers,
his hope that they'd lead to peace.
But all I heard was his chesty voice,
gazed at his moistened lips.

I was sealed in my own hormonal launch
hurtling through space, gravity
lifted off all my neurons. I orbited
beyond my rooted sphere,
moonstruck at how Mr. Briggs
and the vast reaches of men
I knew had fathered kids.

Our class soon learned that *Sputnik*
sparked an accelerated space race, but I
wouldn't activate my inklings
that fast. My capsule
shielded me from a breathtaking
universe I'd just begun to observe.

For the next few years I hovered
head down, still spaced out.
Panting. A lot like Laika.

# barrel-girl

these days, she must scrunch
to squeeze inside her barrel
leaving room around her light
that she hides in there

not her sylph-like self
but what swirls within her head
& sings through her voice
strains the barrel's slats
tests the iron rings
that restrict its width

she presses knees &
elbows closer to her chest
reposes in the dusky glow
& never craves expanded space
nor lifts her light outside
to sparkle with the sun

# antlered man

*from Stephan Balkenhol's sculpture "Man and Stag"*

few would hoist themselves onto a stag's antlers —
even with the stag stock still, high on a bronze table
you could heave yourself up to the stag's broad
bronze back, then ease between its antlers

but if you choose to slip into the antlers' curved
branches, you can lounge above floor-bound
pursuits, your view shared not even with the stag
who stares off to your right, while you gaze ahead —

as you laze in smooth-boned antlers, let one
brace you halfway up your back, rest
your right knee in the other's notch, your left
leg straight so the antler's crook will prop it

settled on your private perch, you'll sit tall, face
dim to those below, thoughts your own —
now that you've clambered here, you could always
slide back down, but why?

# Night mare

I was sure she knew the way
before I climbed astride her.
Yet she froths as if pursued,
shuns her turn down the lane,
refuses to veer at the bend.

The mare swerves to flee the road
and my head snaps back.
Our clear route vanishes.
She carries me through the dark
as I cling to her mane.

She bolts into woods
where high limbs scrape my cheek,
low ones gouge her head.
She blinks oozed blood,

trips over roots and stumps.
I blanch as undergrowth swells,
logs block each footfall.
Still she plunges on, and
I strain to lean with her stride,

brace for each sudden jolt.
But we're at the woods' end.
Her hooves deep in marsh,
I shriek as she rears,
lurch as she sprints
and skids sideways.

Mud shifts to sand.
My eyelids flutter
when the horse halts on seashore
sharp with shells.
Wide-eyed, I clench.

And tomorrow night, if this mare
bounds by, will I let her pass?
Or mount again to search
for my dream's dim shelter.

# Jupiter

*from Mozart's Symphony #41, "The Jupiter"*

in her college music lab's straight chair, the lean
young woman broadens, listening to the Jupiter
symphony, till middle-aged she fills
her red plush seat in tonight's concert hall

the crackly LPs pressed Mozart's sonata form
("stating," "developing," "recapitulating" themes)
so deep within that waning eardrums still
trace the route through "The Jupiter"

Mozart's godlike music develops stately song
soothes minor moments in cloudless finale —
like that young woman on the cusp, oblivious to burdens
her years will bring, then at last resolve

so that now the orchestra's recapitulation
retrieves smooth phrases that resonate
to peel back decades to Mozart's first statement
bursting through headphones from that scratched LP

# Life classes

I disrobe for strangers
who stand at easels.

One woman rips a sheet
from her oversized pad
and sighs. "He doesn't ask
what it's like, stuck
at home all day."

Housewives draw their spheres
and lines freehand, years after
art school, before the birth
of women's lib.

Their charcoal arcs my angles
in broad strokes, dabs detail.
My body static as the clock ticks,
my eyes roam the teacher's 1964
decor. Its structure stripped.

Her front room's bare pine floor,
couch and single square table,
wicker rockers scattered
near bamboo shades.
Slender sansevieria that point
to faint corner light.

I curve my legs along exposed
wood on the sofa frame, sprawl
on its hand-loomed cushions.
Or jut my hip, elbow akimbo.
Maybe press my palms together,
lift my arms up straight.

"Remember when we looked like her?
Then we found Mr. Right
— and this." The woman's thumb
smudges a charcoal shadow.

Toes rooted, head inert,
my mind lurches through her words
that colour this scene.

When clock hands move,
mine do too. I extend
my arms and legs da Vinci-like,
to reach the rims of both
a circle and square.

Time to change my pose.
Through bamboo slits,
sun ruddies my face.

# adrift

whose hubris plunked these
blue dots, yellow arrows, red stars
on back-lit maps
at parks, airports, malls
to proclaim
*you are here*

a spatial illiterate
who can't decode
these symbols
of my whereabouts,
I'm cast out
to roam
till humans
or landmarks
unscramble the way

my memory
semi-literate,
I recall bare themes
but few details
such as whether to buy
hand or dish soap
or which bend
in the bike path
steered me
*here* just now

a text-literate
who seeks narrative
that leads far
beyond words,
I confront the quandary
of why, in fact
I am *here* right now
in this park, at this mall
on this earth
this Tuesday afternoon at three

on behalf of all lost souls
who can't align themselves
with *here* blazoned on bright signs,
smug sign planners
please humour us,
add a lone letter
so we feel at home
as we wander
and ask ourselves
*you are where?*

# outside quotidian time

I
snow falls in feathered flakes
laughter flutters as passers-by push stuck cars

along the street people seem weightless
even women with thickset legs

my own steady step drags to a standstill
will my knees carry me home?


II
muted evening holds my yard
in pearled glow from a hazy moon

I remove mounds of snow from my car
though I have no plans to go out tonight

on the crab apple branch above my head
red fruit buds sit dotted with snow

# paper punch holes

my gaze straight ahead, I scorned this foreign
student who lived among white circles
*like pressed hail pelting his old ways*

I knew how my world would unfold, while this man
of science grasped nothing, his paper punch holes
*thin white stones on his childhood beach*

spotting floors of this flat he'd soon leave
so it could become my first married home
*where this fairy dust would charm my days*

I foresaw perfect years forever ahead
betokened by these profuse full circles
*like lavish sugared vanilla drops*

still, I planned to sweep snags from my future
so I'd clear out this clutter
*Hansel and Gretel's white-bread crumbs I'd never need*

why ponder this man's 3-hole punch crammed
until its cover burst, its cracks drooling holes
*like sleet he first felt here*

snaking his work trail, spilling through stale air
as fans stirred or windows rose, his circles sprinkling down
*pearly tears for his homeland*

why muse that he'd punched data sheets in files
then flung these remnants, beguiled as they fell
*dandruff from tight papers while his mood was loose*

I, hard-edged like holes locked at 10mm, 3 per page
couldn't see him shape positive from negative space
*with curved blinders shielding my eyes*

soon my marriage would cement my views
why probe gadgets like this man from distant lands
*new to winter's whitened globe*

yet as each married day rolled into my wifely life
qualms like scattered holes clear only as they clustered
*these bland repetitive spheres*

turned dulcet *O!*s to duller pleas against my long constraint
and defecting, I sprawled in holes I'd freshly punched
*bright balls bouncing down an opened road*

at last just like this man I'd met in my artless age
who'd spun punched holes to sense both sides
*their oxymoron of sameness in snowflakes*

# Shortcut

When it all becomes
too much, she trims
her fingernails
to the quick.
Saws their corners
around and across
with a steel file
till they curve
like fingertips.

Her skin on the children's
skin, on her maple
desk. Breath smooth.
She anticipates
the weeks ahead
before she'll approach
a surface again
through shell-like
feelers. Will listen
for their click
of contact. Gouge
her cheek in sleep.
Overshoot
her touchscreen's *I*.

Get a grip
she tells herself.
A grip.

# Vista

A silken road once led languorously to sleep.
Then through the years my feet dug ruts
whose edges ensnare me and block the route.

As I stroll toward deep sleep, crevices
consume my shallow breath, jar my heart
to hammer beats, my mind to chew its fears.

*Two faceless women at the park. Each sinks in quicksand*
*to her throat before she's swallowed whole.*

*Beneath my bed a plastic bag. Slime oozes*
*from the smothered infant stuffed inside.*

*An absent friend extends her neck. On the left*
*an axe descends, sharpened to behead her.*

I'm straddling this road's midpoint bend. Tattered
silk behind, the roadblock still ahead. No detours, stops
or U-turns at this farther end. Each night

a lurch of panic tugs my sights to that next
stretch of road. Shows me my footsteps poised
to shuffle into endless sleep.

# why I write

so at times when my
arteries abruptly explode
veins rip, bones splinter through my skin
lungs screech silently
clamped stomach heaves
brain's vestige slithers down the hall
and my heart
plops beside me on the rug

then my blue ballpoint pen, operating anywhere—
even on thin white paper
in a stippled pocket memo book—
swiftly sedates my neurons
punctures the putrid inflammation
eases each organ back in place
suturing membranes securely
to support this equilibrium
till my mind and innards mend

this blue ink finger points my way through the dark

# half moons

# half moons

my mother, blind on her deathbed
limp hand on the nurse's, palm to palm —

the nurse edges a file
along the arcs of my mother's nails
rounds their tips, compresses their cuticles
brushes clear polish across their surface

*a person's nails continue to grow*
*even after death*, the nurse says

my mother, generic old woman
since shrunken gums collapsed her mouth —

inert in her rented hospital bed
manicured fingers slack on the sheet
their exposed half moons
primed to glisten briefly in her grave

# missing

Dido's final lament in
Purcell's opera *Dido and Aeneas:*
*"Remember me, but oh, forget my fate"*


*Remember me*, Dido pleads as she dies
when Aeneas leaves for other lands —
this aria's dark harmony now pierces
the stone shield my mother
built bit by bit while she lived
to block her own lyric song

Purcell leads me to mourn
my mother's fine voice that never
merged with mine to sing
the music buried on our tongues —
yet could music alone have tuned
flat years of all we left unsaid?

She plunged the sword of silence deep
when my father vanished to his grave —
but while Dido warned us to forget her fate
my mother shaped her own in such long strokes
that even music never raised her minor mood —
so once he was ripped from her heart
what she might have shared became barren art

# compacts

slip of the clasp
click of the crisscross lock
muffled clunk
when mother's
1940s compacts jostle —
sharp snap
as strong clips close

mother opens her nightstand
offers old-fashioned compacts
to her child sick beneath thick quilts

sweet fruit scent —
old powder
puffs in air
when scalloped lids are raised
or hot palms stroke
cool silver sides
etched with fine lines

the child seldom sees these compacts
shut tight in her parents' room
where she knocks to enter

her embellished tales
of fancy balls and teas
connect the compacts
in her make-believe
as she stores their sheen
in pillowed warmth
of her parents' feather bed

she begins to etch her hours and years
with textures, smells and sounds
she shapes to storied lines

# my mother played Chopin while lamb stewed

what a sumptuous scene, you must think—
you hear Chopin's waltz skim piano keys
smell herbed lamb broth that steeps leeks and carrots
sense chords and aroma fuse in the hall
between hushed rooms and the warm kitchen stove
see my mother rapt in melody
even beaming at our upturned faces
as they catch the light

my mother managed Chopin's waltzes
straight-backed, fingernails clicking each key
plunking phrases she labelled *romantic*
though she'd long lost her ardour—
and the lamb stew?
carrots soaked slack, gristly, bland broth
burning off in an acrid puff—
another dry meal in our cold tiled kitchen

but in her way, my mother did slip inside her music
and before we'd heard Ashkenazy play Chopin
we liked her playing, so why would we doubt
she was *high-brow*, as she called herself
back when we still thought her hours
enthroned at the piano explained
the lack of fragrant family meals—
my mother, queen of appearances

# optometrist's daughter

I hinge my reading glasses
on their frame's thin strength:
folded, with lenses away
from hard surfaces

professional wisdom
my father left me
remains
half a century later

*wipe lenses with soft cloths*
*prop sidepieces crossed*
*store glasses in their case*

solid suggestions for
spotless lenses
to sharpen my sight
and

small recompense
for what dimmed
when he disappeared

# Omen

The gong hung by a wire
from the crossbeam between tree trunks cut
in their prime. Assembled as gallows.

In Hangman, the game of letters that foreshadow
words, children watch a body part appear
at each failed turn until a stick-figure looms.

But this gong sprang full-blown
one night. Its rusted edge ripped
summer from our corner ballfield.

                    *

Curved like this gong, my father
bent above my bed to staunch
my dread of the dark intruder.

He bypassed the gong's origin,
duration, even proper name. Diluted
its purpose to soft-edged emergency.

Yet he calmed my foreboding.
With his weight and warmth so near, I touched
his moustache, knew the gong would never ring

nor did it. Though Hangman soon appeared
mysterious as that metallic disk.
Its crisis now my father, whose hard-edged disease

uncapped my fears as he swiftly died.
My world erupted so abruptly
no warning knell could sound.

# After 65 years of work

It seems my father has retired.
His job was being dead.
He didn't choose it, but like most
workers, fell into it.
He'd tried selling eggs,
cleaning houses, a stint
as an optometrist. But I just
remember him as dead.
The job got into his bones

once office life absorbed him.
In another profession,
he'd have stepped down
when his age crept up
to the retirement deadline.
But here, where he's forever
stuck two decades
too young to retire,
he dug himself out
after 65 years in the office.

At last, he has infinite time
for me. He pops up unannounced
at odd hours of the day,
breathless to offset lost years
buried at work. He contemplates
me at my desk, my luminous Mac
as I scroll and click.
My father who was dead

before television's birth
stares at a woman who appears
on my laptop, her face
an aged double of his.
While I Skype with my sister,
he observes the yellow desk
he'd built over our treadle
sewing machine. He studies
his grade school photo grouped
with those of my grandchildren
older than me when he left for his job.

He watches my height unfold
as I stand, my hair gleam greyer
than his in ambient light.
His mouth opens and shuts,
yet I never expected him to breathe
warm words. By now
I know we all need jobs, particularly

a *pater familias* like you
back then, Father. Somehow
you've found me in this cold
country. I welcome
your whiskered whiffs
near my cheek whenever
you arrive. I work at home
and earn my own living.
Like you in the deep years
I knew you, I keep to myself.

# Waiting room

On opposite ends of a vinyl couch:
mother and daughter. An empty
space between them.

The mother (short hair cowlicked)
ventures a word, eyes locked ahead.
Waits for her daughter to turn to her.

Her daughter (hair cropped, cowlick gelled
and bleached) sits silent, gaze forward.
Rummages for her cell phone.

The daughter's eyes (behind square glasses)
don't see her mother's (glasses round).
From my vinyl chair, I watch them both.

Once that daughter (still on land phones)
I'm now sometimes that mother
who glances at her daughter's hand

while she rises alone for the nurse.
The daughter clenches her phone
and waits for this morning to end.

Soon mother and daughter leave
having settled me in their space.
No words among us for what
led to this waiting room.

# Dear Mother

Shall I fling this letter into air
where your life dissolved
in tight-lipped grief fifty years ago
when my father died?

Or shall I hurl it into the earth
where your skeleton
has no membraned eyes to read?

I know these words can't fill
your gaping cranium.
It's twenty years since blood
plumped your brain

and forty since we lived side by side
in solitude. You schooled me
till I understood that you alone
knew true anguish, that my frivolous thoughts
must be swallowed mute.

Now I'll risk this written conversation,
though my fiery childhood eyes
have hardened to embers.
Then why gnaw my pen
to heave these words into a void?

It's just that your bone fingers
could grasp the key
to my chronic quandary:
whether, Mother, I ever loved you.

# Names

*from Charlotte Brontë's novel* Jane Eyre

My mother labelled me marble. Smooth outside,
hard within, she said. Named me Adele:
so rare I startle at others who bear it,
even in fiction or memoirs of the dead.

As if our name branded our traits.
Jane Eyre's pupil, Adele Varens, primps
in clustered curls and a pink silk dress.
Exclaims over porcelain and ivory gifts.

Jane observes Grace Poole's patient
in a lunatic's attic, though Mother needed
no Grace Poole to restrain her. She never
bit me or burned our house, her hollow
madness drier-veined, never named.

Later, she called her bronchoscopy
and thoracentesis medical blows
with fearsome names. Had she beckoned,
would she have seen me soften
during her last disease? We two grown
close as adult Adele Varens and Jane?

It's only in Mother's final diary I learn of
Adele Poole: the hospital room companion
who locks me to Mother beyond
her bloodless end. Like inked footprints,
ellipsis points circle back to her holding me,
newborn, and giving me my name.

# glimmer

*I want oatmeal soup for lunch*, my mother said —
muddled frown-lines marked her face, a winter hat askew

but she couldn't swallow soft food, so I knew
how deeply she'd declined

I felt no urge to cry

later, as storms cut heat to the house, I wrapped my mother
in quilts to ease her ride to a warm motel

I tucked her into the double bed and lay as sentry
on her rug, yet when I woke she slept next to me

at dawn I learned this storm could rage for days

I took my mother to hospital
till I could nurse her at home again

she bristled, almost alert — *if this is a hospital
I won't stay one single night!*

under duress, my mother groped for her lost senses

her bygone hopes seemed to hover in that moment
then sink into the grim times ahead

this glimmer of the person I'd long known
unsealed the sorrow I had stemmed so far

I rounded the corner, out of view, to mourn

I felt my mother merge with the human story —
together we moved into its mortal lore

a stranger's hand touched mine as I hugged the wall
*I don't know why you're crying, but I'm sorry*

I wept for my mother then

# Passion

> *Ruht wohl, ihr heiligen Gebeine,*
> *Die ich nun weiter nicht beweine.*
> *Ruht wohl und bringt auch mich zur Ruh!*
> —final chorus of Bach's *St. John Passion*, performed at Easter


Look who's brought me rest. Our choir voices surge:
*Rest well, o sacred limbs.*

*We need not weep for you.* My breath implores the earth
to ease my prolonged sorrow.

> My inner voice sings to my father's bones, buried
> young, and to my mother's: buried old,

> half her years lost mourning. Seared by his absence,
> she'd long orphaned my soft flesh.

> Now as Bach braids the Passion's grief in tight
> restraint, the troubles of my blood unknot.

Serene strains resonate to smooth my veins,
his measures scored so I absorb tranquil chords.

I hear the music through my parents' ears. Each reprise
hews deeper till this sarabande transforms me. In harmony

of woodwinds, choir and strings, my Jewish parents,
indifferent to Easter, arise to redeem me.

# Moorside Blend

# math for couples

**diminished:** $1 + 1 < 2$

she had no socks
so she wore his

that left him short of socks
so she bought him more

**equated:** $1 + (1 + 1 - 1) = 2$

the young woman snared
an older woman's lover

the jilted woman warned
we're the same, just different seasons

**augmented:** $1 + 1 > 2$

she said I love you even
with your string tie

he said I love you even
though you don't like my string tie

# marriage, Canadian-style

*from Mozart's opera* Zaïde

okay, maybe not *marriage*
maybe not even *plighting our troth*
let's just say *public declaration*
that fits our Canadian union
no church clap-trap
not even government rhetoric
just my radio message
that wafts coast to coast
proclaims my love for you

Zaïde sings her love to Gomatz
in the opera with her name
four discs of this calm aria
from your music collection
announced on CBC Radio 2
across Canada
and beyond

we share our music
with peers this morning
Emma Kirkby sings
on the airwaves
at my request, for you
while you and I
listen together
in our front room
breathing with Zaïde
as if we sat with Gomatz
here on our couch
wrapped inside their song

# hot flesh

you touch me &
my flesh heats up —
flashes of pleasure
zap my brain
surge through
my core —
menopause meets seasoned sex

you tinker till
my circuits cool
buzz & hum
while we recharge —
our ebbing flesh
overhauled in
doze with dual snores

I rise & grope
for bifocals
then brew sweet tea —
samples from the health food store
where I buy herbs
to stave off ills
middle-aged women are prone to

# ash-blonde

my blatant wig first turned your eye toward me

late that night, no downy, straight or wavy hairs
hid my bare skin's paleness, tawny flecks
or soft expanse around my torso

my blemishes, surface and ingrown, waited in your sight

coquettish courtship games were futile for us —
I was unable to expose just my beauty marks
then one by one shyly reveal my moles and warts

through my head's bald skin you read my grief

before that night, I'd scurried deep inside my wig —
floundered alone, since no one cared to peer within
my coiffed vinyl helmet dyed garish red

then you approached to warm me with your breath

later, as we showed friends and neighbours
the ash-blonde wig you'd given me
a smooth lustre plumped my cheeks and bathed my lips

deftly you dissolved my conspicuous shame

I gazed at everyone directly, my face smartly framed
by someone's real grown hair —
*did you know?* I could ask at last

now slowly we've restored the brick house you bought us

we've peeled our oak kitchen's sturdy bones
cushioned them with our mingled sinews
covered their skin in quiet colours of our days

the entwined patterns of our nights

most of my life I'd searched for shelter —
hand in hand, we still needed two full years to find
our home, where now that you encircle my *I*

a place to live grows into our place to love

# arm wrestle

take any good guy — warm, witty, well-read, kind ...
would never help himself before ensuring you have yours
but put him on an airplane, seat him at a film
his elbow spears the armrest

you hunch your shoulders, bunch your elbows at mid-waist
request a bit of armrest to stretch your rounding back
he's cramped, he says, with nowhere else to put his arm
*I know* you scream inside as your bones scrunch even more

you nudge his mind — partners, fair play, parity ...
he withdraws, you conquer briefly till he reasserts his grasp —
you shove, sheepish, prepare to set up siege
then seize the prize as he leans across to hold your hand

# notes on musical lines

we share soft chunks of fudge
chocolate-orange, chocolate-pear
dark fruited sugar strands spinning through
my harried arteries and veins
unwinding inner wires to five lines
that evenly transect my inner spaces

knotted nerves had blocked
my view of loosened ways, till today
ambling down an open track, you
led me to this limestone inn, through wide halls
to this feather bed near its wood fire
fed me red wine and now, these sweets

*every good boy deserves fudge*
I murmur, my tones in treble clef
muscles unravelled as music staves —
you respond, your bass clef voice
resonant in support of our duet
*good boys deserve fudge always*

# Huckleberry friend

*lyrics thanks to Johnny Mercer*

After ten years of words, you mention
your high school prom. Insist you felt fine
there alone. Its theme *Moon River* —
that year's hit song.

We're deep in our seats at the Towne Cinema.
Screen dark before the feature, a short film
spools between the ventricles of my heart
and brain. A 1961 crepe-papered gym.
You bunch with other boys who never cross
the floor, gorge on chips.

I invent a prior scene. Your Sears shirt
top-buttoned, slide rule holstered to your belt.
A math class where you blurt
your rehearsed invitation. What might I
have said? Would I have seen through
your glasses to your quiet eyes?

I could have worn my pink tulle dress
with thin-heeled satin pumps dyed to match.
We'd have danced stiff-armed, weak-kneed.
Small talk stumbling, though already
we were *after the same rainbow's end.*

But who knows what I would have said.
No violins or soft focus: just my close-up then
and now. That dress from my own prom
still in my closet. After the movie, I try it on.
The waistband no longer fits.

# spring cleaning

just jettison old hurts —
why wash and press them
sheathe them in plastic
arrange them in your drawer

heave them out for Sally Ann
whose fresh gaze
oblivious to your grievous wrongs
highlights their bright spots
forgives fades and stains

but if some ground-in grudges
lodge under your skin
you can always soak them
so their sticky edge dissolves
or rinse their dark creases
till your veins run clear

then flap your woes in rapid wind
shake loose their dusty tears

# "Be it ever so humble, there is no place like home"

Be home-like! ... no place ever. So, "humble:" there it is.
It is there, like so. (*Ever humble*) No place, be "home"?
Ever be there, home! No humble place is so like it.
So be humble like no place there. Is it ever home?
"Humble" is, like, so *there*! Ever! Home it! No place? Be.
There is! So be home (no humble place ever). Like it?
Is there no place like it? Ever? So be humble, home.
No, like home. Humble place, be ever there! It is so.
Place it like home is. There! So! No, be humble ever ...
Like, *so*? Be humble, there. No place ever home? It is.
Home is there, ever. Humble. Like no place. So be it.

# Matrix

*Webster's New World Dictionary definition, with 7 sections*

| West End Cleaners Receipt | | |
|---|---|---|
| **Tuesday** | **1 Rug** | **N/P** |
| Brought in Tuesday, | green square rug. | Normal price. |
| 1) Mathematics: | set of terms arranged in rows and columns | between parentheses or lines |
| Tuesday is when | we'll finish one carpet | and the next piece. |
| 2) Linguistics: | main | or independent clause |
| To drop off Tuesday. | Gold shag runner | at our new place. |
| 3) Geology: | earthy material in which a fossil | is enclosed |
| Deliver on Tuesday? | Since your carpet is large, | that's never possible. |
| 4) Electronics: | process that combines signals for transmission, | then separates them for reception |
| By Tuesday, | you'll bring a hand-loomed mat to square the corners? | Fine, if it's not plush. |
| 5) Printing: | metal mold for casting, plaster etc. impression | from which a plate can be made |
| After Tuesday, | pick up your area rug with sheepskin lining. | Should be no problem! |
| 6) Anatomy: | nonliving substance in which living cells | are embedded, as in bone, cartilage etc. |
| [ma·trix (mā′triks) — | just | my tricks.] |
| 7) Archaic: | womb; | uterus |

# weekened

when's the day I'll no longer
thirst dazed for those
fried aphids I once ate as I
sat, urd deigned in
sun dated by that hairy bean
mundane in its season, and I
too staid to parlay more

# yatter

(sign on a fence —
*win a cake*
*whack a piñata*)

kin awake
pack what ya oughta

yah, wake a yawner
pin her if ya gotta

yak yak, you're yin
to your yang daughter

one cracked wacky yap
yadda yadda yadda

opaque patter

# jam

you get just one
piece of toast to spread it on —
still, you try to take as much
jam as you can

you do your best
to grab your slice from
the middle of the loaf
but whatever size slice you get
— even if you're stuck
with the puny heel —
here's the decision you face

should you spread all
your jam over the whole slice
so each bite has the same
flavour and sweetness?

or use just enough
so each bite leaves
a slight jam taste
then pile what's left
on your very last bite
— rich and thick and sweet —
since the last is the one
you'll remember?

# Moorside Blend

*at Moorside, the Mackenzie King Estate*
*in Gatineau, Quebec*


mid-September, autumn should be settling in
but the day belies statistics — lawn's expanse
still summer lush, lavender-centred petunias
hot-pink begonias overflowing urns

this porch with its green awning borders
long-needled pines, spruce crowned in cones
and full-leafed maples tinged with red
above the slope to faux-antique stone ruins

we sip Moorside Blend to toast the date
we first shared tea, which flowed mint hot
from a brass teapot's spout — now our
afternoon tea plate, tiered like a wedding cake

presents us with shaved-radish sandwiches
and capered smoked salmon triangles
then dark chocolate wedges on its middle plate
with scones for clotted cream on top

you rise, take your camera
and circle birches while I savour tea —
thick paper napkin drinking ink for this poem
where Mackenzie King gazed at his grounds

amid worn wood smells, rustle of high maple leaves —
only bittersweet air reminds us summer has gone
this coda a gift like our verdant life
whose season would have us cool with our years

# snapdragons

grey November morning:
frost has sapped
plants' vibrant green
leaving bleak beige stalks —
blanched their upright strength
to aqueous wan algae —
yet through a chain-link fence
wine-red, mixed-yellow
deep and fairer pink
snapdragons strain towards the sun
bloom, and prosper

# Notes

Italicized headings in "Sorehenna: *as her, none*" are anagrams of "Sorehenna."

"Aristotle's friend" is based on Aristotle's *Poetics.*

# Acknowledgements

Thanks to the editors of the following journals, where earlier versions of some poems in this book first appeared.

"half moons" in *The Antigonish Review*
"missing" in *Ars Medica*
"signature" in *Bywords*
"snapdragons" in *Bywords Quarterly Journal*
"barrel-girl," "granddaughter, age 3," "Greek island legacy" and "welcome" in *Canadian Woman Studies*
"why I write" in *Contemporary Verse2 (CV2)*
"lexicon of travelling light," "on seeing Picasso's 'Woman in a Hat with Flowers,'" "paper punch holes," "Sorehenna: *as her, none*" and "Waiting room" in *The Dalhousie Review*
"Swee-Touch-Nee" and "tonic" in *Parchment*
"outside quotidian time" and "spring cleaning" in *Qwerty*
"arm wrestle," "ash-blonde," "Grandmother's mountain meadow," "Jupiter," "math for couples," "October 5, 1957" and "Vista" in *Room*
"harmonious arc" and "lightly up and over" in *Vallum*
"anatomy ↔ genealogy," "Be it ever so humble, there is no place like home," "coordinates" and "jam" in *White Wall Review*

Thanks to Natalie Ventura, whose poetry writing showed me the way. Thanks also to Rona Shaffron for friendship and warmth in the writing community. I am grateful to Stuart Ross, and to Peter Richardson, David O'Meara and Mark Frutkin for their advice and guidance. And thanks to David O'Meara for launching my book at Plan 99 in Ottawa.

Many thanks to Michael Mirolla for his belief in this book and for publishing Canadian poets in his Essential Poets Series.

Special thanks to my sisters Florence and Natalie, daughters Erica and Joanna, and grandchildren Anna, Ben, Kaia and Cora for their part in the saga. And thanks to Ed, always.

# About the Author

Adele Graf grew up outside New York City and immigrated to Canada in 1968. She has worked as a writer and editor, and taught writing in the public and private sectors in Halifax and Ottawa. *math for couples* is her first book of poetry, though more than half the poems in this book have been published in Canadian journals including *The Antigonish Review, CV2, The Dalhousie Review, Room* and *Vallum*. She lives in Ottawa with her spouse.

Printed in March 2017
by Gauvin Press,
Gatineau, Québec